Old CURRIE, BALERNO & JUNIPER

by
George Monies

This picture of a carter from Juniper Green is a reminder that transport in the area still relied on horse and trap until the First World War. Perhaps this was the equivalent of the modern taxi!

© George Monies, 2001
First published in the United Kingdom, 2001,
by Stenlake Publishing,
Telephone / Fax: 01290 551122

ISBN 1 84033 163 1

FURTHER READING

The books listed below were used by the author during his research. None of them are available from Stenlake Publishing. Those interested in finding out more are advised to contact their local bookshop or reference library.

Malcolm Cant, *The Villages of Edinburgh, vol. 2*, 1987.
John Geddie, *The Water of Leith from Source to Sea*, 1896.
Stuart Harris, *The Place Names of Edinburgh*, 1996.
Stanley Jamieson (ed.), *The Water of Leith*, 1984.
Graham Priestley, *The Water Mills of the Water of Leith*, 2001.
Donald Shaw, *The Balerno Branch and the Caley in Edinburgh*, 1989.
John Tweedie, *Currie in Old Picture Postcards*, 1983.
Water of Leith Conservation Trust, *A Guide to the Water of Leith Walkway*, date
    unknown.

ACKNOWLEDGEMENTS

Many people have contributed to this publication, but I would particularly like to thank the staff of the National Library of Scotland Map Library and the City of Edinburgh Public Libraries, especially those at Currie and Balerno. Much needed technical advice was provided by David Thomson.

   The book is dedicated to the memory of my mother, Sadie Monies, and to Helen and Paul.

These semi-detached houses at Blinkbonny, Currie, may have been built for mill managers or foremen. It looks as if there may have been a local golf interest!

INTRODUCTION

The communities of Currie, Balerno and Juniper Green on the west side of Edinburgh are linked by the Water of Leith – Edinburgh's river. They are also linked, to the south, by the Pentland Hills. Transport too has connected them – the Lanark Road (the 'old turnpike'), which runs alongside the river, and the railway, which for almost one hundred years, also kept them together.

Currie derives its name from a number of disputed origins. From 1210 it was spelt 'Curey' and then went through a variety of spellings until it became Currie in 1410. The most likely explanation of its origins is that it comes from similar Gaelic names meaning a 'hollow' or 'corner'. There can be little doubt that Currie's position on the Water of Leith was not accidental. It was a 'ferm toun', but inevitably the fast flowing river was to encourage manufacturing by the use of mills. Balerno, as a settlement, has been recorded since 1280 but appears to have been called Balharnoch (Gaelic – *baileairneach*), meaning 'a farm or steading with sloe bushes'. By the seventeenth century a place called Byrney stood on the site and there is reference to a barley farm there. The name survived through the Byrnie Paper Mill, built in 1799 and now gone, and some locals still refer to Balerno as 'Byrnie'. As with Currie, Balerno's position on the Water of Leith tied it with mills.

The origins of the village of Juniper Green are more obscure. A farm of that name is recorded in the eighteenth century presumably referring to the presence of juniper in the area but there is little or no evidence, from the records, of any juniper. A more likely explanation is that it derives from the presence of juniper on the coat of arms of a John Murray of Polmais whose daughter married into the local landowning family, the Cunninghams of Woodhall. 'Green' seems to refer to a bleaching green in the Curriemuirend (east) side of Juniper Green. There is little doubt that the settlement was a much later development than its two neighbours but it too owes its growth to its position on the Water of Leith.

Although the Water of Leith is the main river in the area, a tributary – the Bavelaw – runs from the Harlaw Reservoir through Balerno to join the Water of Leith. A number of mills were situated on this stream to the south-east of Balerno. The purpose of these mills gives an indication of the occupations in the area – threshing, beetling, spinning and paper-making. On the Water of Leith itself the oldest recorded mill (1376) is Balernoch Waulk Mill, a cloth processing mill. From the most upstream mill, Leithhead, to the boundary of Juniper Green at Gillespie crossroads, the mills had a variety of purposes and were involved in the making of barley, grain, glue and snuff amongst other products. Whatever their origins these mills were mostly converted to paper-making in the eighteenth and

nineteenth centuries and some of these continued on until the mid-twentieth century.

Despite the manufacturing on the Water of Leith, the area remained largely agricultural. Local estates remained the main source of employment for the population and these estates gave rise to many of the local names. Amongst the landowners can be included the Skenes of Curriehill, the Scotts of Bavelaw and Malleny, the Craigs of Riccarton and the Cunninghams of Balerno. Perhaps the largest of these estates was Riccarton which included the lands of Currie. The Riccarton estate now houses Heriot Watt University and many of the present-day residents of the three townships are connected with the university.

Being so close to Edinburgh, it is not surprising that Currie, Balerno and Juniper Green have histories that are both local and national. The early Stewart family had connections with the area. Mary, Queen of Scots, apparently enjoyed hawking in the neighbourhood and her son, James VI, built stables for his horses near Bavelaw Castle where he was a frequent visitor. In the seventeenth century the area saw involvement in the Covenanting wars.

Robert Louis Stevenson's grandfather was minister in the neighbouring parish of Colinton and Stevenson's first published book was about the Covenanters' battle at Rullion Green. The story has it that escaping Covenanters found food and sanctuary in the moor behind Bavelaw Castle and that their dead were buried at the old Harlaw Farm. It is said, too, that Burke and Hare, the bodysnatchers, met in a Balerno inn. In Currie there was also a local poet, a weaver called Jamie Thomson, who was a contemporary of Robert Burns. His name is commemorated in Currie with Poet's Burn and Poet's Glen and in Thomson Road. Another local dignitary was Sir James Gibson Craig, a leader of the Scottish Whigs in the nineteenth century and friend of Cockburn and Jeffrey. For a time, Thomas Carlyle and his wife lived in Juniper Green in an attempt to escape from the hurly-burly of Edinburgh.

The development which transformed these settlements into an urban setting was the railway. In 1874 the Caledonian Railway Company opened the Balerno branch on its main Edinburgh–Glasgow route. The line left the main route at Slateford and crisscrossed the Water of Leith through Colinton, Juniper Green, Currie and Balerno to join the main line at Ravelrig Junction. This link with Edinburgh was to make the three villages attractive to the city's growing middle class. Previously they had built villas in the area for summer use, but now they were able to live in the area and commute as it took only thirty-one minutes on the train from Balerno to Edinburgh Princes Street. For a time, too, the railway renewed the life of the mills as it allowed them access to a wider market. However, the growth of motor transport was to hit the railways and consequently the mills as well. Passenger transport declined and the branch closed during the Second World War. Freight transport continued until the 1960s, but the closure of freight transport spelled the end for the mills. Most of them have now gone, replaced by small industrial estates or private housing. Currently the main activities in the area are connected with the needs of residents of these 'urban villages' and the nearby Heriot Watt University.

The three communities are included now as part of the wards of Edinburgh City, Balerno and Baberton. The latest population figures are about 8,000 for each. Comparisons are difficult because of boundary changes but the population of Currie Parish (then in Midlothian), which included most of the area, was about 2,000 in 1841. It is now quite distinctly 'commuter land'.

Riccarton House, Currie, was extended by Sir James Gibson Craig in 1874. The original land was given by Robert the Bruce to his daughter Marjorie in 1315 on the occasion of her marriage to Walter, the High Steward, thus originating the Stewart dynasty. By the fourteenth century the estate was owned by the Wardlaw family who helped to found St Andrews University. In the seventeenth century it came into the hands of the Craig family and by the nineteenth century passed to the Gibson family. After the Second World War the house was used as General Headquarters Scottish Command, but was demolished in 1965. The estate became the site of Heriot Watt University in 1966.

VILLAGE FROM THE STATION, CURRIE.

This was the centre of the old village. The more recent developments are over the hill. The station was the only one on the Balerno branch of the Caledonian Railway to have two platforms, the remains of which can still be seen on the Water of Leith Walkway. The river is hidden between the station fence and the cottage. The remains of the Currie Mill kiln are still standing. This was a grain mill which dated from 1506 and ceased operation in 1854. Note how sharply the railway line turned to cross the old Currie Bridge. The photograph dates from about 1920.

CURRIE

This is Lanark Road West looking towards Edinburgh. The house to the right, which is still inhabited, was the old post office. The house next door was the telephone exchange. Mail for England was taken from here to Curriehill Station where it was picked up as the train to London passed on the Edinburgh–Glasgow line.

CURRIE COTTAGES, CURRIE

To the left of this view of Lanark Road West are early farm cottages. The later cottages, to the right, are distinguished by porches. Despite the fact that the chimney of Kinleith Paper Mill was built high enough to disperse smoke, this obviously depended on weather conditions. It was the fifth largest paper mill in Scotland and at one time employed four hundred people. It opened in 1792 and ceased operation in 1966. There is now an industrial estate on the site. Amongst the trees to the left was a bakery and a grocer's shop, each with stables for delivery vans.

Lanark Road West looking east about the turn of the century. The house straight ahead is the old toll house. Behind the trees is Kinleith Paper Mill which also supplied gas for the street lights (to the right). The road down led to Currie Bridge. The cottages to the left still exist. One of these was the cartwright's workshop. The gable is that of Riccarton Arms Hotel. The tollhouse was demolished to make way for the main road to Edinburgh.

Another view of the village from the station. The Water of Leith is more prominent here as is the mill kiln. To the left of Burnside cottage was a field where farm animals were pastured while awaiting transportation on the railway. The prominent building behind the kiln is Society Hall which was built in 1831 by the Currie Friendly Society. The Society invested its money in the turnpike roads and used the profits to pay families sickness and death benefits. The building served as committee rooms and a hall. It was demolished in 1965 to make way for road widening. To the right of society hall is the Turlies and above that is Easter Currie Farm, both of which are still occupied as private residences.

In the centre of the picture is the fourth (Board) school of Currie, built in 1903. It is now the local library. Opposite this was the first school which opened in 1699 and was originally three cottages. To the right is Riccarton Arms Hotel which until 1874 was Wester Currie Farm. The cottages next to this still exist and are scheduled to become an extension of the hotel. Amongst the buildings to the left was the smiddy. One of the blacksmiths, Mr Stark, was used as a model for the famous oil painting of 'The Thin Red Line' at the Battle of Balaclava by Robert Gibb. Strangely enough, the timber telegraph poles still carry telephone lines.

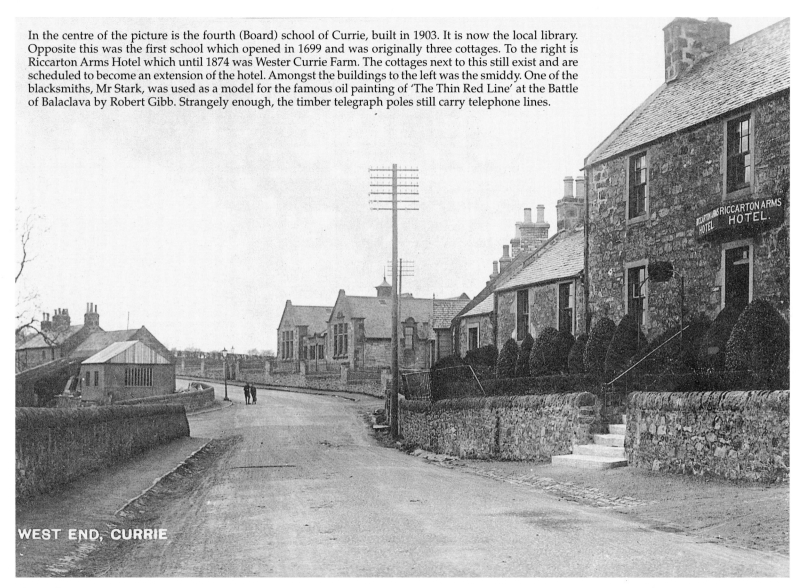

WEST END, CURRIE

Main Street, looking west. This position was once called Toll Corner. In the centre is Riccarton Arms Hotel. To the left is Society Hall, while on the right is Easter Currie Farmhouse. Behind the tree is now the present Post Office. In front of this is a monument to the famous Everest mountaineer Dougal Haston who came from Currie.

This excellent photograph gives an idea of old Currie. To the left is the old school and schoolhouse, built in 1820. To the right is the second school of 1824. To the front is Currie Bridge which dates from the sixteenth century. To the right of the bridge can be seen the chimney of the miller's house. Across the river from this was St Mungo's well, so named because one of the ministers of Currie Kirk became Principal of the University of Glasgow, St Mungo's city. Running over the bridge is the branch railway. There were no Sunday trains on the line until 1913.

Currie Kirk and schoolhouse. The kirk was built in 1784 on the site of older churches which dated back to the fifteenth and sixteenth centuries. During reconstruction to the east of the church, stones dating back to the thirteenth century were found. Each featured circled crosses, two of which had swords. The previous churches were the seat of the Archdeans of Lothian and they were known by the village's older name of Kyl-de-leithe. The schoolhouse was opened in 1829 but is now a private dwelling. One of the schoolmasters designed sundials which were eventually presented to Currie Kirk.

2564 Balerno Station.

Balerno Station was the terminus of the Balerno branch line. The line served the four mills in Balerno. That passengers were a secondary consideration was proved by the line's closure in 1943 and its continuation as a freight line until 1968. On the left is the stationmaster's house.

BALERNO

This is a view from what is now Bridge Road with Balerno Church. The field to the right was called the Long Braes and is now the site of a housing estate. The primary school and library, built in 1878, are to the left of the road. The house is Larchfield and is still inhabited. The wall extended on to Balerno Bridge over the Water of Leith. A few yards to the left of the photograph the Bavelaw Burn joins the Water of Leith.

This is Main Street looking north. To the right is the edge of the offices of Balerno Bank Paper Mills. The cottages to the left were for farm labourers and are now gone. The gable wall (above the cart) is that of Malleny Arms. During the Second World War it was frequented by American troops from the nearby Kirknewton camp and the hotel became known as 'The Honky Tonk'.

This is the entrance to Balerno Bank Paper Mill. The offices were in red sandstone and the logo above the entrance door is J.G.C. – John Galloway Company.

Originally built in 1805, Balerno Bank Paper Mill was a combination of three mills – Byrnie, Townhead and Balerno Bank. A siding from the Balerno branch transported the mill's raw materials and finished products. It burned down in 1909 but was redeveloped from 1924 by the John Galloway Company and became very successful as the photograph indicates. Workers were even transported from Edinburgh. It was demolished in 1989 to make way for housing, although the red sandstone offices were retained as flats.

This is Main Street looking south. The single storey cottage is now the local bookmaker. Down from this was the White Horse Inn (now the Grey Horse), the meeting place of Balerno Burns Club and the reputed meeting place of Burke and Hare before going on their local explorations. At the top of Main Street was the local co-operative, founded in 1866, and this area was ironically known as Society or 'Happy Land' – so-called because the residents fought over the use of the washing line. At the top is the offices of Balerno Bank Paper Mill.

There were two mills here on the Bavelaw Burn. The first was built in 1805 and processed flax while the other, built in 1825, made sail cloth. The first later became Spink's Bung mill which made wooden bungs for beer barrels. It burned down in 1954. The 1825 mill was used for a time as a school for local children with the teacher living in the lower section. After this it became a grain mill. The mills were demolished and the whole site is now taken by housing.

MALLENY, BALERNO

Farm buildings abound in the area despite the industry of the mills. The Scott family held the Malleny estate for many generations, supplying soldiers, lawyers and ministers to the locality and to Scotland. Although the family's members had professions, until the mid-nineteenth century their wealth lay in the land and farming. These buildings are typical of farm steadings for cattle and pigs and there is still a pig farm in Currie. The sheep were pastured on the nearby Pentland Hills.

Lymphoy House, Balerno

The Lymphoy estate dates back to the sixteenth century. Some maps show a Lymphoy Castle which probably dated from the fourteenth century, but this building is an extension of Easter Lymphoy farmhouse. The name is probably Celtic – 'lom' meaning bare and 'fa' meaning a place. Near the house excavations have revealed that there seems to have been a burial ground there, dating from about AD 500. At some point in the past, attempts were also made at copper mining in the area but they came to nothing. The ruins of Lennox Tower are nearby. James VI presented this to the Duke of Lennox and it was also the home of the Archdeans of Lothian.

This estate dates from the fourteenth century and was originally owned by Thomas de Hill. It was known as 'The Hill' before it became Curriehill. In the fifteenth century it was part of Mary of Guise's land. Some of the revenues from this estate contributed to the foundation of Edinburgh University in 1583. Alexander Wardlaw, an owner of the sixteenth century, was one of the murderers of David Rizzio. Other owners included the Watsons who helped to found George Watson's College in the seventeenth century. The house, inhabited in the nineteenth century by the Lords Curriehill, judges of the Court of Session, had idiosyncratic features like the chamfered chimneys and a round gable. The present house is a small portion of the original which had almost one hundred rooms.

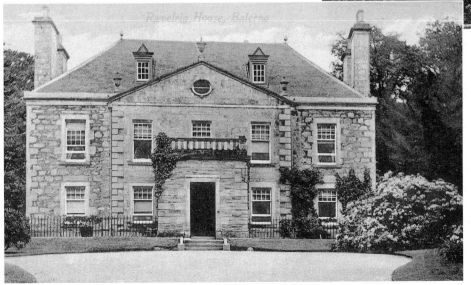

Ravelrig has had various spellings but seems to mean a fenced field. The estate dates from the fifteenth century. In the seventeenth century it was owned by a famous Edinburgh doctor, Arthur Temple, who performed a remarkable operation on a women by removing a horn from her head – shades of witchcraft perhaps! It is said that the results of this operation were displayed in Edinburgh University but are now lost. The estate and house were eventually owned by Lord Ravelrig, a judge of the High Court. The policies include a large walled garden and an eighteenth century doocot. The local hunt left from Ravelrig House. The house eventually became a Barnardo's children's home, but is now sadly derelict.

ALBANY SERIES 4191.

UNITED FREE CHURCH, LANARK ROAD east
JUNIPER GREEN.

Lanark Road, looking west. Before the Disruption of the Church of Scotland in 1843 worshippers had to travel to either Colinton or Currie. Disruptionists of the Free Kirk had a meeting in Currie's Society Hall to demand a church and in 1845 a feu was obtained from Sir William Foulis to build a new church. This small church was replaced in the early 1880s by the present church which is distinguished by its twin towers and belcote. Before it was consecrated Mr Gladstone, leader of the Liberal Opposition (and later Prime Minister), addressed a meeting there during his Midlothian Campaign in 1879. At consecration it was named Juniper Green Free Church. In 1900 it became Juniper Green United Free Church and after unification with the Church of Scotland in 1929 it was known as St Andrew's Juniper Green. It is now Juniper Green Parish Church.

This is the west end of Juniper Green at the junction with Belmont Avenue. At the far end of the photograph is Enterkin's Yett (gate) and the boundary with Currie. The building to the left with the tall chimney is Juniper Green Co-operative Society.

Another view looking east. The main building was Juniper Green Co-operative Society, later renamed St Cuthbert's Co-operative. The building to the immediate right has been demolished and the tall chimney has gone. All the other buildings still stand.

BELMONT AVENUE, JUNIPER GREEN

Belmont Avenue seems to have originated around 1845 and took its name from a path from Woodhall Park. The position of the camera marks its junction with Lanark Road near Enterkin's Yett which was named after the landowner John Cunynhame of Enterkin in Ayrshire. It seems he constructed a gate at the point where Lanark Road entered Juniper Green. The small building to the right, still in use as a residence, was the village smiddy. The name Belmont was taken from a dairy in the street. The street name was changed to Juniper Avenue in 1967.

Looking east again. The building to the left is still a grocer's although it's now under different ownership. The coach with the tophatted coachman may have been that of Dr Graham, the local doctor. His coachman, Johnny Davidson, was a local character.

The south side of Lanark Road. At the top of the photograph is the west gable of St Margaret's Church. The house with the street gable was originally Woodhall Dower House, later becoming St Margaret's manse. It is now a private house.

LANARK ROAD. JUNIPER GREEN.

This is the junction with Baberton Avenue on the left. The grocer's shop at the corner still stands but is no longer a grocer's. To the right is Station Road, leading to Juniper Green Station. The station closed in 1958. St Margaret's Church was built in 1895. Previous to this, Church of Scotland members used an iron church on the north side of Lanark Road. In 1974 it was decided to amalgamate the congregations of St Margaret's and St Andrew's and the latter became the parish church. Subsequently, St Margaret's was demolished and houses for the elderly are now on the site with one of the stone crosses from the church positioned at the entrance to the block. St Margaret's Church hall has been retained as a function hall for the complex.

Baberton Avenue, Juniper Green.

This was the southern approach to the Baberton estate. The white building at the top is the primary school of Colinton School Board and is now a nursery school. To the left of this was the Volunteers' Hall (the Volunteers were the equivalent to today's Territorial Army) and then the Young Men's Club. To the right, coming down the hill, the single storey building was originally the Female Subscription School which, before 1872 and the introduction of state grants for schools, was paid for by fees. It is now a private residence. Most of the other buildings still exist, including the shop at the corner.

Woodhall Drive, Juniper Green.

No1

Running parallel and to the east of Baberton Avenue, Woodhall Drive was a development of the 1930s. The Woodhall estate encompassed most of Juniper Green. To the left of the council block is Juniper Lodge on Lanark Road. Torphin Quarry, now closed, is in the background.

W.R.&S. 24701. CURRIEMUIREND JUNIPER GREEN.

Curriemuirend was the traditional entrance to Juniper Green from the east. It was originally a thirty-two acre farm and steading. The name derives from its position at the east end of Currie Muir. The area has almost all been replaced by the City Bypass. All that remains are some houses in Viewfield Road and Muirend Avenue.

There were many pedestrian bridges across the Water of Leith. This one led to Juniper Green Station by the path to the left. To the right, the pathway led to Woodhall Mains and the Woodhall estate.

Lanark Road looking east with St Margaret's Church in the distance. The Railway Inn, which has been in business since the railway arrived in 1874, is in the middle distance.

The east end of Lanark Road just before the parish church. Behind the distant trees is Lorimer Lodge which is now a nursing home. All the other buildings still stand, having been built for Victorian commuters. To the immediate left is a house called Mount Parnassus (the home of the poet gods of Greek mythology) in reference to Jamie Thomson.

EAST MILL NEAR JUNIPER GREEN

491 55

The area was a complex of three mills and is, technically, in Currie. The view is from Mutter's Bridge. The near buildings are those of Wylie's farm. Behind these buildings was a snuff mill with a distinctive building overhanging the river. On the left was East Mill Bank which was a barley mill. The ruins of this mill can still be seen but the other mill building has gone. Behind both buildings was the bridge carrying the railway.

PENTLAND TERRACE
JUNIPER GREEN

These appear to be mill and quarry worker's houses on Pentland Terrace. They are one-up, one-down with entrances to the upper houses by a stair and balcony at the rear. The houses date from before the First World War. The gardens have been replaced by parking spaces and the walls are now harled. Pentland Terrace is now called Juniper Terrace.

WOODHALL HOUSE, JUNIPER GREEN 491/50

Woodhall has existed from the fourteenth century as part of the barony of Redhall, but as there is no evidence of a house here at that time 'hall' would appear to have originally referred to a haugh – thus the 'haugh at the wood'. The estate was extensive, encompassing most of Juniper Green. The house, however, dates from 1630. It has been added to over the years, but now contains individual flats. Woodhall House once contained the Bannatyne Manuscript, a two volume collection of Scottish medieval poems by Dunbar and Henryson. This is now in the National Library of Scotland.

Baberton lodge is the building beyond the gates. It is now the clubhouse of Baberton Golf Course. The estate was originally named Kilbaberton. The Golf Club was started in 1893 as a nine-hole course and then extended. It has fine views of Edinburgh Castle and the River Forth. The club lays claim to the birthplace of the steel-shafted golf club. The frontage of the lodge has now been disfigured by a modern extension. There are still survivors of the avenue of trees and the stone columns still exist.

Baberton House was built in the seventeenth century on the site of a medieval tower. The builder was James Murray, James VI's Master of Works. It is reminiscent of Heriot's Hospital in Edinburgh. The house has changed hands many times, once as the result of a lottery ticket. From the south it is approached by a long avenue from Baberton Lodge. The house has now been converted to offices.

PENTLAND HILLS. FROM WOODHALL TERRACE, JUNIPER GREEN.

This photograph is of the houses in Woodhall Terrace which runs parallel to Lanark Road. The transept windows of St Margaret's Church can clearly be seen. To the south is Torphin Quarry. Stone from the quarry was used for many of the houses in the area and the quarry workers lived locally.

FROM TORPHIN JUNIPER GREEN

Torphin was also known as Lady Burn after the stream which leads from the Clubbiedean and Torduff reservoirs. The neighbouring hill is Torduff or White Hill. In the foreground is Torphin farm.

There were four mills on the Juniper Green stretch of the Water of Leith. This was the smallest. During their lifetime, the local mills produced a variety of products including snuff, grain, paper, board and glue. All water-powered mills had similar characteristics. Upstream was a weir which could divert the water to a lade and, being narrow, the lade increased the flow to power the mill wheel. Many mills, like this one, had farms attached which were usually run by the miller and his family.

JUNIPER GREEN

Because of the numerous mills on the river there were many weirs. This one, which can still be seen behind the site of Juniper Green Station, is distinctively L-shaped. The railway line lay behind the wall.

United Free Manse, Juniper Green, Midlothian

The manse of the United Free Church lay east of the church on Lanark Road. It was next to the old bowling green. One of the ministers was Rev. Norman Macfarlane who served for thirty-five years and saw the gradual uniting of various Disruption churches until the final amalgamation with the Church of Scotland in 1929. When the City Bypass was built, the bowling green was moved but the manse survived.

SNUFF MILL JUNIPER GREEN

The East Mill was developed from 1749 by Abraham Ferrier and James Thomson. It was the first snuff mill on the Water of Leith and produced, amongst other brands, cinnamon snuff. The railway ran behind the wall and the wooden bridge led to East Bank Mill. The mill was closed in 1920 and demolished.

SNUFF MILL, JUNIPER GREEN.

Watt's snuff mill lay in the heart of Juniper Green behind St Margaret's Church. The right hand rails led to Juniper Green Station and the left hand rails to the goods sheds. The mill operated until 1940.

Despite the industrial nature of the mills the area was, and is, agricultural. The substantial farm cottages were fairly typical – lit by oil lamps and with little heating except a coal or wood fire, and not a long way from the middle class luxury of the New Town! The two-horse plough was a late nineteenth century improvement on the single horse, as was the steel plough. These fields saw many a ploughing match.